BRITISH RAILWAYS
STEAM
IN RETROSPECT

The Post-War Era

Eric Oldham

The History Press

First published in 1998
This edition first published in 2009

The History Press
The Mill, Brimscombe Port
Stroud, Gloucestershire, GL5 2QG
www.thehistorypress.co.uk

British Library Cataloguing in Publication Data.
A catalogue record for this book is available from the British Library.

ISBN 978 0 7524 5018 6

Typesetting and origination by The History Press
Printed in Great Britain

CONTENTS

The driver of A4 Pacific no. 60028 *Walter K. Whigham* awaits the signal to depart with a King's Cross–Leeds express at Peterborough, 1958.

INTRODUCTION

After the Second World War Britain's railways comprised four railway companies which were nationalized to form British Railways on 1 January 1948. This photographic collection records the last two decades of the steam locomotive as modernization of the railways gave way to diesel and electrification projects.

Remarkably, many vintage steam locomotives of pre-grouping origin had survived the war and this feature may be noted in the collection. After the introduction of new standard designs of steam locomotives from the BR stable in the 1950s, these proved to be the last of the line and had a comparatively short life. The final steam locomotive to be built on British Railways was BR 9F 2–10–0 no. 92220 which was appropriately named *Evening Star*. It was subsequently preserved for posterity and may now be seen in the National Railway Museum at York.

The photographic content of this book is arranged under nine different themes relating to railways and may serve as a reminder of days past, when a whistle down the wind indicated not only the approach of the 10.15 a.m., but a way of life.

Chapter One

CREWE STATION AND LOCOMOTIVE WORKS

When the railway came to Crewe it had only thirty inhabitants. It was here in 1843 that the Grand Junction Railway established its locomotive works on a site occupying 2½ acres. Three years later, however, the Grand Junction was amalgamated with the Liverpool and Manchester, the Manchester and Birmingham, and the London and Birmingham to form the London and North Western Railway.

It was under the new regime that the railway centre of Crewe developed on the grand scale before subsequently coming under the control of the London, Midland and Scottish Railway in 1923, and latterly British Railways London Midland Region in 1948. The vast complex of Crewe has interested students of railway history for over 150 years. This selection of photographs illustrates the railway scene and also some of the products which were built at the locomotive works before the introduction of the modernization plan in 1948.

Memories of Crewe include the footbridge at the northern end of the station which provided a favourite viewing gallery for countless enthusiasts, the vast amount of postal and parcels traffic, and the splendid tea rooms, not forgetting the NAAFI canteen which, in wartime, provided solace and refreshment for the many thousands of service men and women who 'changed at Crewe'.

Stanier Pacific no. 6232 *Duchess of Montrose* with a Glasgow–Euston train at Crewe in the autumn of 1946. The locomotive has survived the war in the attractive red livery of the LMS and sports the distinguished large gilt numerals.

Unrebuilt 'Royal Scot' class locomotive no. 46113 *Cameronian* is observed shortly after nationalization in 1948, whereby former LMS steam locomotives had their individual numbers increased by 40,000. The locomotive has retained the original parallel boiler.

This panoramic view of the northern approaches to Crewe depicts a Chester train departing behind a rebuilt 'Scot', 1955. Behind the locomotive is Crewe north junction signal-box which has survived to this day as part of the Crewe Heritage Centre. The main lines to Liverpool and the north are straight ahead, and the lines radiating to the right are to Stockport and Manchester.

Stanier Pacific no. 46203 *Princess Margaret Rose* stands on the centre road at Crewe in 1955 with the through Plymouth–Glasgow coach awaiting arrival of the Down 'Mid-day Scot', which it will take over for the more strenuous part of the route to Glasgow.

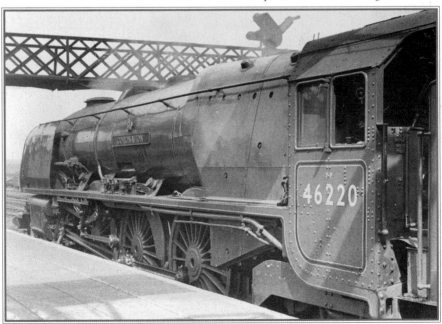

Stanier Pacific no. 46220 *Coronation* stands at the north end of Crewe station with the Down 'Royal Scot' in 1951. Formally streamlined, the locomotive is adorned in the early BR light-blue livery which was adopted for some of the larger passenger locomotives before the familiar BR green livery was introduced as standard.

A relief train to Manchester arrives at Crewe from the south behind unrebuilt 'Patriot' no. 45505 *The Royal Army Ordnance Corps* with a varied selection of rolling stock, 1948. It was here on 29 June 1937 that the *Coronation Scot* made a dramatic entrance after attaining 113 m.p.h. just 2 miles out from this location.

Unrebuilt 'Scot' no. 46156 *The South Wales Borderer* approaches Crewe from the south with a through train which is formed of an interesting array of rolling stock, 1948. The locomotive portrays the early BR livery of black with red, cream and grey lining which was used on secondary passenger and mixed traffic engines, blue being selected as first choice for the largest express classes at this time.

A West of England–Manchester train awaits departure after 'Jubilee' 4–6–0 no. 45581 *Bihar and Orissa* has been attached for a running in turn, 1955. In the background is no. 46201 *Princess Elizabeth* returning to shed after bringing in the Up 'Mid-day Scot'.

Great Western 4–6–0 no. 6877 *Llanfair Grange* is observed at Crewe south in 1949, waiting to proceed to the station where it will be attached to the afternoon train to Wellington.

'Saint' class 4–6–0 no. 2854 *Duckenham Court* backing down to Crewe station for the afternoon train to Wellington in 1947. The GWR presence at Crewe disappeared during the period of electrification, and the Wellington service was withdrawn on 9 September 1963.

Stanier Pacific no. 6225 *Duchess of Gloucester* reposes on the ashpits at Crewe north shed in 1947. This locomotive was streamlined when built ten years earlier but this was removed in the early postwar period, revealing the sloping smokebox of unusual contour.

An imposing study of Stanier Pacifics at Crewe north shed, viewed from the roundhouse, 1951. Locomotive no. 46253 *City of St Albans* in green livery stands majestically by the turntable on which is positioned a Midland Compound 4–4–0. On the right is Stanier Pacific no. 46235 *City of Birmingham* painted in the experimental light-blue livery of the early BR period.

Stanier Pacific no. 6227 *Duchess of Devonshire* after de-streamlining reposes at Crewe works in the postwar LMS livery and displays the tapered smokebox which was a feature of these locomotives, 1947.

In the last year of the LMSR, Stanier Pacific no. 6201 *Princess Elizabeth* emerges from Crewe works after overhaul, painted in the postwar livery, 1947. The locomotive made two record non-stop runs between London and Glasgow in November 1936, running northbound in 353½ minutes and southbound on the following day in 344¼ minutes.

Rebuilt 'Scot' no. 6115 *Scots Guardsman* stands outside the paint shop in 1947 and displays the postwar livery of black, lined out in maroon and straw. No. 6115 was the first of the locomotives to receive smoke deflectors.

LNWR 0–4–2 Crane locomotive no. 3248 was a Crewe works departmental locomotive and is shown on the scrap road in 1947. The metal-faced wooden buffer beam is of interest.

One of the survivors of a once numerous class, Webb LNWR 2–4–2T no. 46658 is observed at Crewe works after overhaul in 1948. It has received its BR number but retains the previous ownership on the tank sides. Classed 1P in the power ratings, it is fitted for push and pull working.

The last of the London and North Western 4–4–0s, 'Precursor' class 4–4–0 no. 25297 *Sirocco* awaits its fate after withdrawal in 1949. In the rear are no. 6004, rebuilt 'Claughton' class, and the last of the 'Prince of Wales' 4–6–0s.

No. 6004 was the last of the LNWR 'Claughton' class express locomotives and survived the war in LMS red livery, having been rebuilt with larger boiler by the latter company. It is seen here in 1949.

This LNWR Webb coal engine belonged to a class of some 500 locomotives which were built between 1873 and 1892. It is observed at Shrewsbury (LMS) in 1947. The vintage weather vane is of interest.

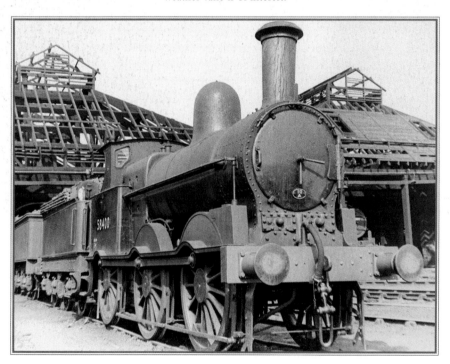

No. 58400 was a former LNWR 18 inch goods locomotive which were nicknamed 'Cauliflowers'. The engine is observed at Springs Branch MPD Wigan in 1948. These locomotives were built between 1880 and 1902 and the last survivors ran until 1955.

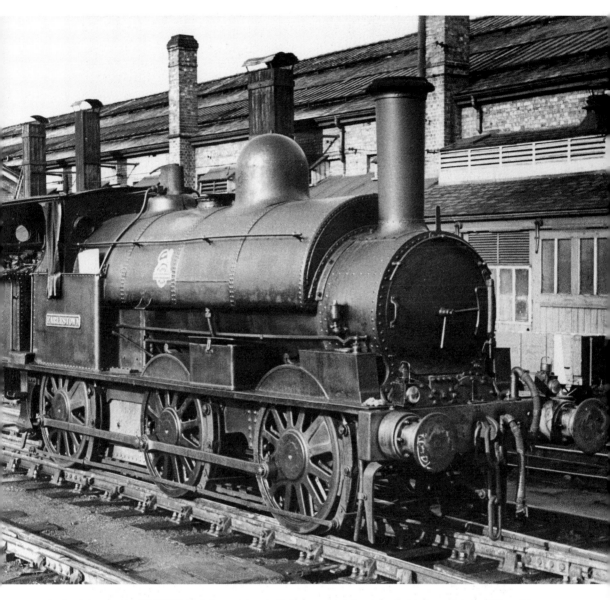

A pleasing portrait of LNWR 0–6–0 special tank *Earlestown* recently ex-works and sporting the BR emblem at Wolverton carriage works, 1950.

A line-up of shunting locomotives at Wolverton carriage works, 1950. In the centre is LNWR Webb 0–6–2 coal tank no. 58887; the other two locomotives are 0–6–0 special tanks of 1875–9 vintage also designed by F.W. Webb.

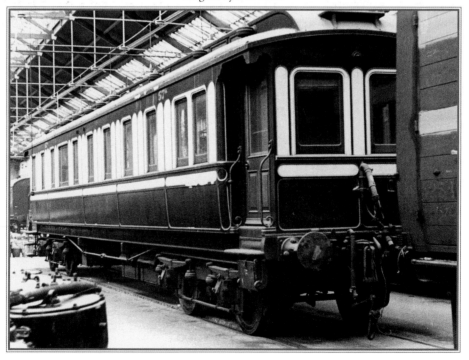

An interesting vehicle observed in the carriage works, 1950. Resplendent in LNWR-style livery is the Duke of Sutherland's private saloon.

Chapter Two

DONCASTER WORKS AND RAILWAY CENTRE

T he locomotive and carriage works of the Great Northern Railway were completed in 1854 and situated adjacent to the junction station of Doncaster, the wagon works being situated at Carr, 2 miles to the south. From its inception, the locomotive works, or plant as it was locally known, was responsible for a range of locomotives that were to serve the east-coast route with distinction.

After incorporation into the London and North Eastern Railway in 1923, the works produced a series of modern locomotives for the various tasks involved to the design of Mr H.N. Gresley. For his services as Chief Mechanical Engineer to the LNER he received a knighthood in 1936 in recognition of his achievements, which culminated in the streamlined high-speed trains of 1935/7 and he was described in *The Times* as 'speeder-up to the LNER'. As a gesture by the company, the hundredth Pacific locomotive was named *Sir Nigel Gresley* in his honour.

The Doncaster works open day was a regular annual event, which was well patronized by the public, with examples of the latest locomotives and rolling stock being assembled for display, together with rides on various improvised contraptions for the children, and other festivities, the proceeds of which went to hospitals and other good causes.

Finally, St James's bridge situated to the south of the station provided a superb vantage point for action photography, and several arrivals and departures of interest are recorded in this selection.

A nostalgic moment caught on camera as an employee at Doncaster locomotive works gives the finishing
touch to a pristine *Mallard*, newly restored to prewar condition for the annual open day.

At the centenary exhibition of the locomotive works in 1953 several 'rides' were popular, such as this crane hoist, where a wagon was raised to a good height, giving an unparalleled view of the exhibits.

Centenary exhibition of the locomotive works, 1953. All the fun of the fair is apparent in this view of an 'improvised' train which gave pleasure to people of all ages and conveys the general bustle and atmosphere of the event.

On Sunday 26 November 1950 the last of the GN Atlantics no. 62822 made its final journey to Doncaster to be broken up. The train, which had commenced its journey at London King's Cross, encountered fog in the Home Counties and was twelve minutes late at Huntingdon, but after breaking through into clear weather made a punctual arrival at Doncaster. The photograph shows the locomotive entering the works for the last time.

To celebrate the centenary of Doncaster locomotive works a special steam-hauled train was run from London King's Cross hauled by the two preserved Atlantics no. 990 *Henry Oakley* and no. 251, here observed from St James's bridge, Doncaster, in 1953.

This picture shows the return Ivatt Atlantic special prior to departure, waiting at the south end of Doncaster Central in somewhat foggy conditions, 1953. The locomotive is 'Peppercorn' A1 Pacific no. 60123 *H.A. Ivatt*.

The return 'Plant Centenarian' leaves Doncaster for King's Cross behind A4 no. 60014 *Silver Link*.

At the rear of the second 'Plant Centenarian' of 27 September 1953 was this streamlined beaver-tail observation car which was used on the 'Coronation' express from 1937 until the outbreak of the Second World War. This view shows the interior decor.

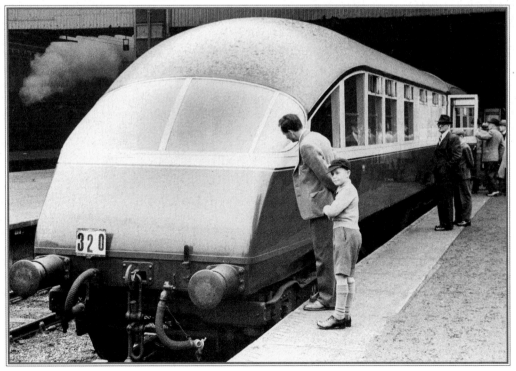

A general view of the observation car at King's Cross on arrival with the 'Plant Centenarian', 1953. It has lost its LNER livery of Marlborough and garter blue and is painted in the early BR livery of red and cream.

A4 Pacific no. 60007 *Sir Nigel Gresley* makes a spirited departure from Doncaster on 23 May 1959, when it achieved a speed of 112 m.p.h. on the descent from Stoke summit with a Stephenson Society special to King's Cross.

A4 Pacific no. 4468 *Mallard*, shortly after restoration, is the star attraction at the Doncaster locomotive works open day, 1960s.

Stainless steel emblem attached to A4 Pacific *Silver Fox*, 1953.

A former LMS 'Duchess' class Pacific leaving Doncaster for King's Cross on an enthusiasts special in June 1963. The locomotive is no. 46245 *City of London* resplendent in BR red livery.

Chapter Three

FREIGHT TRAFFIC

Before the demise of fossil fuels for public consumption, goods traffic in the age of steam was prolific, long hauls of coal from the various collieries being a regular feature of operations. These made slow progress on their journeys to the major conurbations, and were made up of four-wheeled wagons fitted with three link couplings and handbrakes, and were often side tracked on to refuge loops so as not to delay passenger traffic.

In contrast, most trains of perishable traffic were fitted with vacuum brakes throughout and travelled at higher speeds behind mixed traffic locomotives. At the other end of the scale was the daily pick-up goods which visited most small towns and, more often than not, had as its motive power some vintage freight locomotive from a bygone age.

Towards the end of steam operation in the early 1960s, however, many main line express locomotives had been replaced by diesel traction, and alternative work such as freight haulage was found for some survivors before their inevitable demise – a case of how the mighty have fallen.

'Johnson' class 2 0–6–0 no. 58192 was a Midland design of 1875 and is observed with an agricultural train en route for Sheffield, having just left the main line at Chinley south junction, 1953. About thirty engines of the class were still in service in 1961.

A former London and North Western 0–8–0 freight locomotive climbs the gradient out of Crewe and passes Madeley with a train of timber, 1951. The class originally consisted of 502 engines, but 275 were still running in 1955.

A Stanier 8F 2–8–0 freight locomotive near Winwick Junction, no. 48268, 1953. It was one of a class of some 663 locomotives, the first of which emerged from Crewe in 1935. During the Second World War many were produced by the other companies for the war effort.

A busy scene at Marple Wharf Junction as a Midland rebuilt 'Johnson' 3F 0–6–0 no. 43273 is about to pass Stanier class 5 4–6–0 no. 45031 on a heavy freight working, 1953. A fine Midland double-arm signal can be observed in the background.

A panoramic view of Chinley in the heyday of steam, 1953. Dominating the foreground is a locomotive turntable, and on the left alongside the goods shed is an interesting pre-grouping passenger brakevan body used as a mess van. Taking centre stage is a Fowler 0–6–0 on a train of coal empties, which was a common feature of operations in steam days.

A freight train between Hyde and Woodley stations on the Great Central and Midland Joint line in the great freeze of 1947. The locomotive is an austerity 2–8–0 produced during the Second World War and a LNER brakevan brings up the rear.

The Retford breakdown train proceeds south hauled by a Robinson GC 2–8–0 no. 63905, 1953. The two ex-passenger brakevans were probably used on main line Anglo-Scottish traffic in the late 1880s.

A Horwich built 2–6–0 no. 42871 passes Marple Wharf Junction with a train of coal empties under supervision of the former Midland signal box, 1955.

A4 Pacific no. 60030 *Golden Fleece* hustles a fitted freight past the level-crossing keeper's cottage near Grove Road, south of Retford, 1955.

After the end of the Second World War in 1945, the LNER decided on an ambitious scheme of painting all locomotives, with the exception of the A4s, in apple green. Here is a rare sighting of class K2 2–6–0 no. 1732 in the new livery passing Retford in 1947.

Class O2 2–8–0 no. 63940, a development of the original Gresley three-cylinder locomotive of 1918, proceeds south at Retford with a train of coal and is approaching the well-known crossing south of the station, 1955.

A former LNWR 0–8–0 freight locomotive brings a coal train through Chinley north junction bound for the Manchester conurbations, 1953. Coal wagons fitted with handbrakes and three link couplings were the norm at this time.

A southbound fish train fitted throughout with vacuum brakes makes rapid progress through Bawtry, hauled by B1 4–6–0 no. 61394, 1955. These Thompson two-cylinder 4–6–0s with 6 foot 2 inch driving wheels were built between 1942 and 1950 and replaced many elderly pre-grouping locomotives.

An unusual sight at Gamston, south of Retford, 1955. A4 Pacific no. 60028 *Walter K. Whigham* makes steady progress with a substantial loose coupled freight.

How have the mighty fallen? Towards the end of steam working, several express locomotives were to be found on mundane duties. 'Royal Scot' 4–6–0 no. 46140 *The King's Royal Rifle Corps* ambles through Crewe with a train of empty freight wagons in 1960.

Chapter Four

STATIONS

T he most memorable impressions of the steam age were to be observed in some of the larger railway stations, where, in the great iron halls, beneath the tracery of the overall roof, the effects of sunlight and steam presented a spectacle of pure theatre. This was pictorialism in its more graphic form. Platform ends could be of interest, but none was so dramatic as at Liverpool Lime Street or Glasgow's Queen Street, where the railway entered a tunnel. Here, at the appointed hour, the daily ritual of departure had an air of expectancy.

In this selection of photographs, the smaller railway stations have not been overlooked. Of the examples depicted, those of Earlestown (Liverpool and Manchester Railway) and Beverley (North Eastern Railway) deserve special mention because of their historical interest.

Railway departures have long been a favourite aspect of film producers, and many an emotional scene has been played out over the years, enveloped in steam and mystery.

It is in such an environment that these photographs record the day-to-day working of our railway stations, when steam reigned supreme in the 1950s.

A Down Plymouth train arriving at Exeter St Davids in 1947, the last year of the Great Western Railway. The locomotive is no. 6002 *King William IV*, one of a class of thirty engines which handled traffic between Paddington and the West Country.

The preserved Midland Compound 4–4–0 no. 1000, newly restored to original condition, reposes in York station on the occasion of its first public run from Birmingham, 1959.

A special train to Swindon before departure at Birmingham Snow Hill, 1950s. The centre of attraction is the famous Great Western 4–4–0 no. 3440 *City of Truro* which once reached a speed of 102 m.p.h. with an Ocean Mail special near Wellington in 1904.

Bangor station, North Wales, situated between two tunnels, is the setting for this pictorial appraisal of 'Jubilee' class 4–6–0 no. 45582 *Central Provinces*, 1955.

No. 50455 was the last of a class of seventy-five Lancashire and Yorkshire 4–6–0s of Hughes design built between 1908 and 1925. It is seen at York on the occasion of its last journey in 1950.

The Sunday diversion of a King's Cross–Edinburgh express creates local interest as the train passes Lincoln hauled by A4 Pacific no. 60034 *Lord Faringdon*, 1955.

A Leeds–Kings Cross express makes a cautious approach to Peterborough north station in charge of
A4 Pacific no. 60030 *Golden Fleece*, 1958. On the left is a Great Northern somersault signal which has been
converted to lower quadrant operation.

Journey's end. Stanier Pacific no. 46230 *Duchess of Buccleuch* basks in the early morning sun at Glasgow Central after bringing in the overnight express from London, 1960.

No. 46241 *City of Edinburgh* raises the echoes as it leaves Glasgow Central with the morning train in Birmingham, 1960.

In the atmosphere of Glasgow's Queen Street station a crowd of spectators has gathered to witness the departure of a special train to Fort William, 1960s. The locomotive is class K4 2–6–0 no. 61995 *Cameron of Lochiel* which was making its last journey before withdrawal from service.

The premier 'Red Rose' express reposes in Liverpool Lime Street and attracts attention prior to departure for London, 1955. This train was usually entrusted to Pacific haulage, the locomotive on this occasion being no. 46255, *City of Hereford*.

York station viewed from the footbridge, 1947. On platform nine is a King's Cross–Newcastle train composed of new LNER corridor stock designed by Edward Thompson. On its way to the LMS south shed is a 'Jubilee' class 4–6–0, and surmounting the scene is a fine North Eastern signal gantry.

A study in curves at Perth as observed from the Dundee platforms, 1963. Of interest in the centre is the morning Aberdeen–Glasgow train in charge of A4 Pacific no. 60019 *Bittern*.

A Pullman train from London King's Cross shortly after arrival at Sheffield Victoria, 1959. The cars are of traditional design and are painted in the familiar chocolate and cream livery; some of them carried feminine names.

The arrival of the 'South Yorkshireman' at Sheffield Victoria, 1959. Mail is unloaded as the engine crew are relieved after their journey from London Marylebone. A passenger savours the activity on the footplate.

Manchester Central station opened in 1880 and was used jointly by the Midland, Great Northern and Manchester, Sheffield and Lincolnshire railways who formed the Cheshire Lines Committee. This view from the 1950s was taken from the concourse. The station is now an exhibition hall.

Liverpool Lime Street in the days of steam. On the left, passengers are entraining on the 'Red Rose' express to London as a class 5 4–6–0 simmers in the background. The motor vehicles reflect the 1950s.

Birmingham New Street in the early 1950s provided all the ingredients for pictorialism. This atmospheric photograph of the great station was taken before modernization in 1967, when it was completely rebuilt.

One of the most historical station buildings which has survived to this day is the splendid original Liverpool and Manchester Railway example of 1830, and is to be found at Earlestown in Lancashire. It is seen here in 1959; the canopy in particular is exemplary.

Beverley station on the former North Eastern Hull–Scarborough line has a fine example of the overall style of roof which afforded good protection from inclement weather. Of pleasing design, it was a feature of many North Eastern stations. The station is seen here in 1965.

A Newcastle–King's Cross express enters York station from the north under the tracery of the overall roof, in charge of 'Peppercorn' A1 Pacific no. 60128 *Bongrace* which was one of a class of fifty locomotives, 1959.

A summer evening at Carlisle. Pacific no. 46257 *City of Salford* stands on the centre road awaiting the arrival of an evening express to Glasgow, 1959. This locomotive was the ultimate member of the class and together with 46256 was an Ivatt development of the design, incorporating roller bearings and other detail alterations.

Before electrification, a local passenger train calls at Hartford in rural Cheshire, en route for Crewe where it will terminate, 1955.

The Victorian façade at the western end of Leeds City station before modernization of the station, 1950. A Stanier 4–6–0 awaits departure as father and child explore the precincts. The platform impedimenta of the period completes the picture.

Chapter Five

STEAM TO WOODHEAD

The former Great Central main line from Manchester to Sheffield entailed crossing the Pennines by way of the Longdendale Valley and Woodhead tunnel, to emerge at Dunford Bridge. It was this section of line that provided the opportunity of capturing on film the day-to-day working of a steam railway before electrification of the route, which was completed to Sheffield Victoria in September 1954, and to Rotherwood sidings early in 1955. On weekdays the line carried a heavy freight traffic, particularly coal, which descended to the north-west conurbations in an endless flow, with empties returning at intervals throughout the day. The Great Central 2–8–0 freight locomotives of Robinson design dominated this traffic over many years, and in the later stages of the electrification work they were to be observed in tandem with the new electric Bo-Bo locomotives operating the coal trains on training runs. The principal passenger services connected Manchester with Sheffield, London, Hull, and Cleethorpes, as well as with Lincoln and the eastern counties. The Liverpool–Harwich Continental boat express ran daily on weekdays in both directions.

Former Great Central F1 class 2–4–2T no. 7097, built in 1889, was one of the last survivors when observed at Gorton in 1946. The class was responsible for working many of the Manchester suburban services.

The Gresley 2–8–8–2 'Garratt' no. 69999 is observed at Guide Bridge as it was about to take a test train to Woodhead after conversion to oil burning. It was withdrawn from traffic in 1955.

Robinson O4 class 2–8–0 freight locomotive no. 3684 at Gorton in 1946 after overhaul. These heavy freight locomotives were employed on coal haulage over the Pennines for many years.

A Robinson O4 class 2–8–0 no. 3646, rebuilt by Edward Thompson after the Second World War with B1 boiler, side window cabs, Walschaert's valve gear and raised running plates, ex-works at Gorton, 1947.

A3 Pacific no. 60103 *Flying Scotsman* excites the gallery as it backs down for the 2.10 p.m. to London Marylebone at Manchester London Road, now re-named Piccadilly, 1952.

A Manchester–Glossop auto-train between Godley and Broadbottom stations is propelled by C14 67447, built in 1907 for the Great Central Railway. It is seen in 1948.

Newly built Thompson B1 4–6–0 no. 1147, spring 1947. It is sporting the postwar livery of apple green and passes Broadbottom with a train from Sheffield to Manchester.

A fine study of a former North Eastern mixed traffic locomotive of class B16 on the descent to Godley Junction, 1948. No. 61443 was one of a class of seventy locomotives which were built between 1919 and 1924.

A Manchester–Hadfield train approaching Broadbottom shortly after the nationalization of the railways, 1946. Class C13 4–4–2T no. 7422 is inscribed with the new ownership. The small prefix E denotes Eastern Region.

A Down freight on the descent to Godley Junction is hauled by Robinson B7 class 4–6–0 no. 1389, 1946. These handsome mixed traffic locomotives were built between 1921 and 1924 and all were scrapped between 1948 and 1950.

In 1948 tests were made with various locomotives to ascertain their performance. Here is the unusual sight of Southern Bulleid Pacific no. 34005 *Bude* on a Marylebone–Manchester express near Hattersley.

The Great Western also made an appearance during the 1948 trials. No. 6990 *Witherslack Hall* rounds the Hattersley curve on its preliminary run before the tests. Note the LNER stock in teak finish.

Great Northern Ivatt Atlantic no. 2885 has turned round on the triangular junction at Dinting in order to proceed back to its home shed at Doncaster so it can pass through the notorious Woodhead tunnel chimney first, 1947.

A former Great Central 'Director' class 4–4–0 locomotive no. 2662 *Prince of Wales* passes Hattersley on a running in trip from Gorton in 1947. In prewar days these locomotives worked the Manchester–Marylebone trains with distinction until the introduction of the B17 'Sandringham' class.

The Manchester–Glossop auto-train arrives at Dinting and is seen on the branch-line platform, in charge
C13 4–4–2T no. 67421, 1950.

A Marylebone–Manchester train approaches Dinting in the early 1950s hauled by A3 Pacific no. 60059 *Tracery*. The rolling stock is in the carmine and cream livery of the period.

Ex-North Eastern B16 three-cylinder mixed traffic 4–6–0 no. 61447 decends from Torside with a mixed freight on a spring day in 1948. Fifty of these locomotives were still running in 1961.

A Great Central B7 4–6–0 on the descent from Woodhead with a Down goods in 1948. The class numbered thirty-eight engines, ten of which were built after the grouping.

B1 4–6–0 no. 61156 on the morning train to Cleethorpes approaches Torside, 1955. Of particular interest is the Great Central 'Barnum' vehicle next to the engine, built in 1910 at Dukinfield.

The Liverpool–Harwich boat express approaches Torside crossing hauled by Gresley K3 class 2–6–0 no. 61877, 1950. This was a formidable working, particularly on this section. The service entailed one train in each direction on weekdays.

Chapter Six

REGIONAL PASSENGER SERVICES

Before the advent of dieselization and electrification projects, journeys by passenger train entailed the use of the many distinguished steam locomotives from each of the former railway companies. Following nationalization of the railways on 1 January 1948 the locomotives of each of the four groups assumed a new identity and livery, together with passenger vehicles and other rolling stock.

The recording of express passenger trains in motion has inspired many photographers over the years. It offered the exponent something akin to the thrill of the chase.

In retrospect, the best results were obtained on gradients, whereby the speed of the train was reduced, and the locomotive effort registered in smoke and steam. The countryside of Britain with its varied landscape provided a satisfactory backcloth to the exercise.

Hot sunny days were ruled out by the perfectionist on aesthetic grounds, as smoke effects were almost non-existent, registering in some examples as a black haze. Spring and autumn, therefore, provided the ideal lighting conditions, the crisp air being instrumental in yielding superb effects of smoke and steam, much to the advantage of the photographer.

The industrial landscape presented a powerful image, and used as a setting for the railway scene, and under appropriate lighting, the effect could be magical.

A Newcastle–King's Cross express approaches Black Carr Junction, south of Doncaster, hauled by A4 Pacific no. 14 *Silver Link* in postwar livery of garter blue, 1947.

A King's Cross–Newcastle train approaches Grove Road crossing, Retford, during engineering work in the vicinity in charge of A4 Pacific no. 15 *Quicksilver*, newly restored to prewar livery in 1947.

Black Carr Junction, south of Doncaster, in 1947 presented a fine array of Great Northern somersault signals. An unrecorded Great Central Atlantic passes on the Down fast line with a parcels train.

Great Northern Atlantic no. 2817 stands at Retford with an evening train to Sheffield, 1947. Originally built in 1904 as no. 288, the locomotive was not withdrawn until May 1950. In their heyday, these locomotives did sterling work on the east coast main line.

In this view of the northern approaches to Retford, A3 Pacific no. 40 *Cameronian* with GN tender is observed on a running in turn to Grantham in 1947. The splendid array of Great Northern somersault signals were soon to disappear after the nationalization of the railways.

An impression of the steam railway south of Grantham focuses attention on the 'Queen of Scots' Pullman, 1960.

The Up 'Flying Scotsman' passes Doncaster in 1947 hauled by A3 Pacific no. 79 *Bayardo*, newly painted in the postwar apple-green livery. The locomotive in the background is A3 no. 60 *The Tetrarch*.

Gresley A3 Pacific no. 36 *Columbo* on Grove Road crossing to the south of Retford during Sunday engineering work on the main line, 1947.

Thompson class A2 Pacific no. 60521 *Watling Street* passes Retford on a running trip to Barkston where it will turn on the triangular junction in readiness for its return to Doncaster, 1948.

A3 Pacific no. 60103 *Flying Scotsman* heads a relief Leeds–King's Cross train through Babworth to the north of Retford on Easter Monday 1948, and affords a sighting of an apple-green locomotive with teak finished stock.

The Great Northern main line near Brookmans Park in Hertfordshire is seen to advantage in this study of a King's Cross–Cambridge train hauled by B17 4–6–0 no. 61637 *Ford Castle*, 1950.

A3 Pacific no. 60092 *Fairway* passes Eaton Wood to the south of Retford with the midday train to King's Cross, 1951. The rolling stock sports the early livery of carmine red and cream of the newly nationalized railway.

A Newcastle–King's Cross train on the climb to Stoke summit after leaving Grantham, 1955. The locomotive is A3 Pacific no. 60059 *Tracery* with GN type coal rail tender. The carmine and cream livery gave way in the later BR period to maroon for main line passenger stock.

On a fine summer's evening the prestigious 'Tees–Tyne Pullman' from King's Cross passes Gamston and makes a rapid descent to Retford with A4 Pacific no. 60021 *Wild Swan*, 1955.

A Sunday Edinburgh–King's Cross train passes Retford in charge of A4 Pacific no. 60027 *Merlin* carrying a headboard normally used on weekdays, 1951. The locomotive is painted in the early BR blue livery and the speed restriction sign is of LNER origin.

A3 Pacific no. 60085 *Manna* in early BR livery descends from Potters Bar with a Leeds–King's Cross train in high summer, 1951.

'Might and Majesty' Gresley A3 Pacific no. 60107 *Royal Lancer*, in its later guise with double chimney and smoke deflectors, climbs out of Grantham with a Sunderland–King's Cross train, 1962.

The elegance of the 'Harrogate' Sunday Pullman' is reflected in this view to the south of Retford, showing the train returning to London King's Cross in early spring hauled by 'Peppercorn' A1 Pacific no. 60134 *Foxhunter*, 1955.

A3 Pacific no. 60040 *Cameronian* is the centre of attraction as it negotiates the High Street in Lincoln with a diverted King's Cross–Newcastle train, 1962.

North Eastern 4–4–0 no. 2342 of class D20 reposes in the bay platform at the northern end of York station in 1947, the last year of the London and North Eastern Railway.

A4 Pacific no. 60026 *Miles Beevor* leaves York for King's Cross with a train from Edinburgh, and passes under Holgate bridge to good effect, 1958. The A4 Pacifics all received double chimneys later in their working lives.

Contrast at Cambridge: ex-Great Eastern 2–4–0 no. 62794 simmers in the bay platform with a local train to Marks Tey, 1955. Alongside is A4 Pacific no. 60008 *Dwight D. Eisenhower* on a semi-fast train to London King's Cross.

Rebuilt Great Eastern 4–4–0 no. 62521 at Cambridge, the tender of which bears the original British Railways insignia. There is also a prevailing GE presence in the signals and the ornately panelled corridor coach. Cambridge locomotive depot forms the backcloth to this scene from the early 1950s.

Cambridge in the heyday of steam, 1955. The express is in charge of rebuilt Claud Hamilton 4–4–0 no. 62576 as a J17 0–6–0 of Great Eastern vintage stands alongside on shed.

Rebuilt 'Scot' no. 46131 *The Royal Warwickshire Regiment* approaches Chinley north junction with the morning express from Manchester Central to London St Pancras, 1958.

A Manchester–Chinley train departs from Strines behind Midland Compound 4–4–0 no. 41048, 1951. This section of line was jointly owned by the Midland and Great Central railways in pre-grouping days.

A Chinley–Manchester train climbs the gradient out of Marple and approaches Romiley, hauled by Midland Compound no. 41066 in early springtime, 1953.

'Patriot' class 4–6–0 no. 45533 *Lord Rathmore* makes a spirited exit from Manchester and passes under a fine gantry of LNWR signals at Longsight with a Birmingham express, 1953.

High summer on Shap Fell as rebuilt 'Patriot' 4–6–0 no. 5512 *Bunsen* climbs to the summit with the evening Manchester–Glasgow train, 1951.

Serene conditions in the Lune valley as a Manchester–Carlisle train approaches Tebay hauled by class 5 4–6–0 no. 45343, 1955.

The Down 'Royal Scot' approaches Tebay from the south hauled by Stanier Pacific no. 46240 *City of Coventry*, 1958. This train, together with the 'Mid-day Scot' and the 'Caledonian' were the prestige services of the west-coast route.

The morning Manchester–Glasgow train negotiates Dillicar straight in the Lune valley in charge of 'Jubilee' 4–6–0 no. 45742 *Connaught*, one of a class of 188 locomotives, 1955.

Great Western 'Star' class 4–6–0 no. 4056 *Princess Margaret* on the occasion of a railtour organized by the
Stephenson Locomotive Society to Swindon works to mark the demise of the class, 1957.

The morning west to north express leaves Teignmouth hauled by no. 6023 *King Edward II* in 1947, the last year of the Great Western Railway.

'King' class 4–6–0 no. 6003 *King George IV* approaches Teignmouth with a Paddington–Plymouth train, 1947. Thirty locomotives of this type were built to handle the heaviest trains between London and the West Country.

A fitted freight is hustled along the sea coast near Teignmouth by 'Bulldog' class 4–4–0 no. 3453 *Seagull* in 1948. It was one of two locomotives of this type surviving at this time.

The Down Torbay Express emerges from Parsons tunnel hauled by no. 6022 *King Edward III*, its final destination being Kingswear on the River Dart, 1947.

'King' class 4–6–0 no. 6023 *King Edward II* passes Cowley Bridge Junction with a Down express as it approaches Exeter St Davids, 1948.

A Plymouth–Paddington express races through Dawlish behind no. 5098 *Clifford Castle* as holiday-makers make their way to the beach, 1955.

'Castle' and 'King' locomotives head the evening postal train to London in 1948 as renovations and improved services were under way in Plymouth under the newly nationalized railway.

The Down 'Pembroke Coast Express' races through Sonning cutting as it approaches Reading behind 'Castle' class 4–6–0 no. 5080 *Defiant*, named after an aircraft of the Second World War, 1955.

The postwar scene at London Victoria after the 'Golden Arrow' service was re-introduced, 1951. The prestigious Pullman express is in charge of 'Merchant Navy' Pacific no. 35027 *Port Line*.

Prelude to departure. An unusual scene captured at the platform end at Victoria. No. 34072 257 *Squadron* of the 'Battle of Britain' class is the centre of attention, 1951.

The afternoon stopping train to Bournemouth leaves Southampton Central behind an immaculate no. 30857 *Lord Howe* of the 'Lord Nelson' class, 1953. The smoke effect was by arrangement, but the slow departure was such that the wind speed overtook the train and blew the billowy white plumes out of the picture.

'Merchant Navy' class no. 35011 *General Steam Navigation* at speed near Shawford in Hampshire with a Bournemouth–Waterloo express. The locomotive carries the light-blue experimental livery of 1951. Note the 'boxpox' driving wheels.

A boat train from Southampton to London Waterloo leaves the docks under supervision of railway employees armed with handbells and flags and cautiously crosses the main road behind 'King Arthur' class 4–6–0 no. 30792 *Sir Hervis de Revel*, 1955.

A portrait of no. 30850 *Lord Nelson* at Southampton Central, 1950. These locomotives were extensively used on the Waterloo–Bournemouth traffic over many years.

'King Arthur' class 4–6–0 no. 30796 *Sir Dodinas le Savage* prepares to leave Brighton with a return enthusiasts train to London, 1950s.

Chapter Seven

MOTIVE POWER DEPOTS AND LOCOMOTIVE SHEDS

S ome of the most memorable impressions of the steam age were to be obtained in locomotive sheds or motive power depots, where under the illumination of the midday sun, atmospheric scenes of light and shade transformed the smoky interior into one of pictorial splendour. Roundhouses, in which stabling tracks radiated from turntables, were excellent in this respect.

The daily tasks to be observed in the shed yard offered further scope for pictures, such as coaling-up and watering the locomotives. Oiling and preparing for the road offered further possibilities.

Surprisingly, many large roundhouses were remarkably quiet and gave one a feeling of awe, the silence being almost cathedral-like, broken only by the simmering of steam and the occasional drip of water. The overriding quality of the roundhouse from a photographic aspect was its atmospheric quality, together with the positioning of the locomotives, and was much more favourable than the more common type of locomotive shed where space was restricted and where the locomotives were arranged in long rows one behind the other.

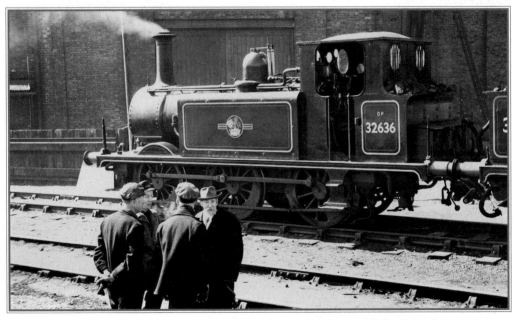

A diminutive Stroudley 'Terrier' class 0–6–0 tank locomotive built in the 1870s for the London Brighton and South Coast Railway simmers in the background as a group of railwaymen talk to a veteran driver of the LBSC at Havant, 1950s.

Gresley K3 2–6–0 no. 61916 in Carlisle Canal shed, 1963. It illustrates the former LNER practice of displaying the class number and home shed on the bufferbeam. Between 1920 and 1937, 193 of these locomotives were built.

No. 7802 *Bradley Manor*, illuminated in the morning sun at Shrewsbury, makes a striking portrait within the confines of the shed, 1958. The class consisted of thirty locomotives.

On the occasion of its last journey before retirement, former LBSC 4–4–2 express locomotive no. 32424 *Beachy Head* is observed on the turntable at Havant, 1958.

Two Gresley Pacifics, rebuilt with double chimneys and smoke deflectors, in Grantham locomotive yard, 1961. They are nos 60067 *Ladas* and 60105 *Victor Wild*.

An interesting scene at Cambridge, 1953. In the foreground is ex-Great Eastern 0–6–0T no. 68625, one of a class of 160 locomotives built between 1886 and 1904. In the background is E4 class 2–4–0 no. 62781, also of Great Eastern vintage.

Fire-lighting equipment for steam locomotives, 1955. Cans of oil and some rather battered shovels used in early morning activity in locomotive sheds.

Class W1 4–6–4 express locomotive no. 60700 at Doncaster, 1955. When built in 1929 it caused a sensation with its semi-streamlined contours and water tube boiler. In the 1930s it was rebuilt on the lines of the A4 streamlined Pacifics, retaining its unique 4–6–4 wheel arrangement to the end of its life.

B1 4–6–0 no. 61237 takes centre stage in this view of Neville Hill MPD and is flanked left and right by two North Eastern J26 0–6–0 freight locomotives, 1958.

Former London and South and Western 4–4–0 of class T9, built in 1899, stands ready for the road at Eastleigh in Hampshire, superbly finished in BR black with red, cream and grey lining, 1955.

The celebrated Gresley A4 no. 60022 *Mallard* poses for the photographer at Grantham motive power depot, 1960. The plaque on the boiler cladding commemorates the attainment of the world speed record for a steam locomotive of 126 mph on 3 July 1938.

Under the coaling plant at Doncaster motive power depot is 'Peppercorn' A1 Pacific no. 60149 *Amadis*, 1958.
This locomotive entered traffic in May 1949 and was withdrawn in June 1964.

'Castle' class 4–6–0 no. 5062 *Earl of Shaftesbury*, recently ex-works, stands outside the locomotive shed at Swindon, 1955. These locomotives were a development of Churchwards 'Star' class.

'Castle' class locomotives nos 5072 *Hurricane* and 5088 *Llanthony Abbey*, the latter fitted with double chimney, at Wolverhampton MPD, 1958. No. 5072 was named after a Second World War RAF fighter aircraft.

A typical roundhouse scene at Derby, 1951. On the left is the pioneer diesel–electric locomotive no. 10000, built in 1947 by the LMS; the other locomotives are Ivatt 2–6–0 no. 43031, Johnson class 3 0–6–0 no. 43546, Fowler 2–6–4T no. 42341 and Johnson class 2 0–6–0 no. 58165.

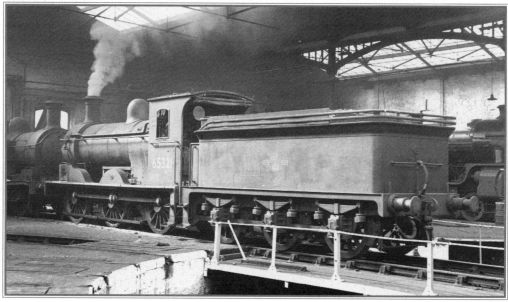

North British 0–6–0 no. 65321 of class J36 at Carlisle Canal depot shortly before closure, 1967. There were 168 of these locomotives built between 1888 and 1900; over seventy of the class were still in use in 1961.

Ex-Lancashire and Yorkshire 0–6–0 no. 52619 at Preston MPD, 1948. This locomotive was a superheated Hughes class 3, rebuilt from an Aspinall design.

An atmospheric portrait of Oxley locomotive depot with a juxtaposition of locomotives, 1955. In the foreground are a 2–6–0 of the 4300 class and no. 4930 *Hagley Hall*.

Akin to a ringmaster at the circus, a lookout man surveys the intrusion of *Flying Scotsman*, doyen of the Gresley Pacifics, into the inner sanctum of Swindon motive power depot, 1960s.

A 2–4–2 tank locomotive of the former Lancashire and Yorkshire Railway at Preston in 1948. No. 50695 was one of a number built between 1899 and 1910.

No. 40383 was the last surviving unsuperheated Midland 4–4–0. Built in 1888, it was later rebuilt in 1909 and was scrapped in 1952. It is seen at Derby works in 1950.

At Doncaster MPD, V2 class mixed traffic locomotive no. 60908 is prepared for the road, the crew replenishing the tender water tank for the tasks ahead, 1955.

A trio of 2–8–0 freight locomotives at Retford MPD, 1960. On the right is a Gresley three-cylinder 2–8–0 no. 63936. On the left is a Robinson O4 class 2–8–0 no. 63655 rebuilt with GNR O2 type boiler, and in the background is GCR 2–8–0 no. 63671.

A B17 three-cylinder 4–6–0 of the 'Sandringham' class no. 61669 *Barnsley* under the coaling plant at Doncaster, 1955. This locomotive was named after a football club, the earlier versions from 1928 onwards being equipped with small Great Eastern style tenders and carrying names of stately homes.

A wartime Austerity 2–8–0 no. 90035 reposes at Doncaster MPD, 1958. Designed by Riddles, this class was constructed in large numbers from 1943 onward.

Stanier class 5 4–6–0 no. 45079 in the BR livery of black with red, cream and grey lining for mixed traffic locomotives, at Agecroft shed, Manchester, 1950.

The Gresley A4 Pacific *Mallard* on the ash-pits at Doncaster motive power depot, 1958. The driver is oiling round as the fireman reads the legend on the plaque on the boiler side.

Gresley A3 Pacific no. 60054 *Prince of Wales* prepares for the road and raises steam at Leicester motive power depot when employed on the Great Central section, 1951.

A former London, Tilbury and Southend 'Intermediate' class 4–4–2 tank locomotive no. 2093 built at the turn of the century at Nottingham, 1947. Seventeen engines of this class survived until 1953.

A Midland Johnson class 5 foot 3 inch 0–6–0 built in 1875, no. 58174 outside a typical roundhouse at Derby in 1950. About thirty engines of this class were still in service in 1961.

An impression of Holbeck locomotive depot, Leeds, towards the end of the steam age when diesel locomotives were infiltrating the system, 1964. Stanier 2–8–0 and 4–6–0s were much in evidence at this time.

York locomotive depot after re-roofing provides a picture of light and shade as workmen attend to their various tasks, 1960s. The building is now part of the National Railway Museum.

A dramatic portrait of York locomotive depot before renovation of the roof provides an atmospheric impression of the steam age, 1947. North Eastern B16 4–6–0s and LNER 'Green Arrow' classes are much in evidence.

A study in light and shade captured at Croes Newydd locomotive depot, 1955. Two class 5 4–6–0s repose in the morning sun.

An improvised oil can (teapot) balances on the connecting rod of a locomotive, 1950.

Croes Newydd provided all the ingredients for picture making, 1960. Sunshine and shadows contribute to the compositional content of this image.

A Sunday morning at Nottingham motive power depot, 1955.

A dramatic picture on the day of the closure of the Carlisle Canal locomotive shed, 1963.

Chapter Eight

SCOTTISH STEAM

I n the early 1960s the Scottish locomotive scene was enhanced by a varied selection of the old and the new. This small collection reflects on some of the survivors from the age of steam.

Of particular interest are the studies of A4 class Gresley Pacifics, which, because of the modernization of the east coast main line, had become redundant, and were drafted to Scotland to work out their lives on the three-hour Glasgow–Aberdeen services. In contrast, Stanier Pacifics were still in command on Glasgow–Euston services at this time.

The delights of Scottish locomotive practice are reflected in some of the scenes, portraying a varied selection of designs north of the border, some of them of pre-grouping origin.

Class 2P no. 40663 is a post-grouping 4–4–0 development of the Midland design. It is seen at Elgin in 1960 when it was used on a Scottish railtour.

K4 2–6–0 no. 61995 *Cameron of Lochiel* was one of six locomotives specially designed for the West Highland line by Sir Nigel Gresley in 1937. It is seen at Crianlarich on its last journey before withdrawal.

No. 62496 Glen Loy was one of the last survivors of the class when photographed at Dawsholm, Glasgow, in 1960. It was designed by Reid for the North British Railway in 1913.

A Reid 0–6–0 J88 dock tank locomotive no. 68346 of the former North British Railway observed at Alloa two years before withdrawal, 1960.

Full house on a North British 0–6–0. This unusual photograph was captured by looking out of the end
window of a passenger brakevan.

The morning express for Inverness leaves Glasgow Buchanan Street behind two Stanier class 5 locomotives. The signal-box is of Caledonian origin, as is the fine lower quadrant signal nearest the camera.

Highland Railway no. 103 was the first 4–6–0 to be introduced in Britain. It is seen on the ashpits at Dawsholm shed, Glasgow, in company with Caledonian 4–2–2 no. 123.

In the 1960s the Scottish Region of British Railways restored four pre-grouping locomotives to working order. Illustrated are the celebrated Caledonian single no. 123 and North British 4–4–0 no. 256 *Glen Douglas* on a return Glasgow–Oban working.

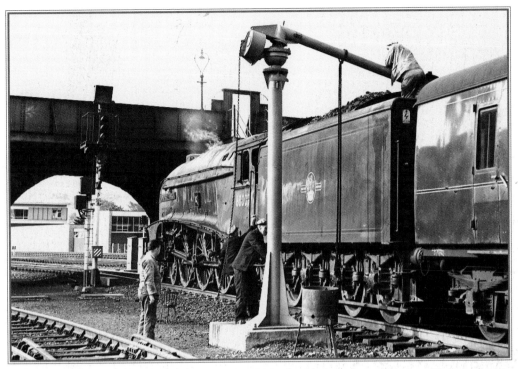

A4 Pacific no. 60009 *Union of South Africa* takes water at Perth with the morning Aberdeen–Glasgow express.

The fireman surveys the road ahead as A4 Pacific no. 60024 *Kingfisher* prepares to leave Perth for Glasgow.

North British 4–4–0 no. 256 *Glen Douglas* on arrival at Perth with a local passenger train.

Chapter Nine

NARROW GAUGE RAILWAYS

The 15 inch gauge Romney, Hythe and Dymchurch Railway was laid across Romney Marsh between the Cinque Port towns of Hythe and New Romney in 1927 and extended to Dungeness in June 1928. The main line to New Romney is double track and the trains are mainly worked by Pacific locomotives based on the LNER Gresley A1 design. The line also has two 4–8–2 locomotives.

The 2 foot 6 inch gauge Welshpool and Llanfair Light Railway was originally built in 1903 and operated by the Cambrian Railway, and was taken over by the Great Western in 1923. When the line closed in 1956 it was taken over by a preservation society and the photograph represents early days under the new ownership. Locomotive no. 1 is named *The Earl*.

In 1950 the Tallylyn Railway Preservation Society was instrumental in taking over the railway after its demise, and the first train ran on Whit Monday in 1951. The society has acquired and restored the original Tallylyn engine of 1865 together with two locomotives rescued from the Corris Railway and an Andrew-Barclay 0–4–0 well-tank locomotive which was one of a pair that spent their working lives at RAF Calshot in Hampshire from 1921 to 1949. The Ffestiniog Railway was built in the 1830s as a horse-worked mineral tramway connecting the slate quarries of Blaenau Ffestiniog with the sea at Porthmadog. In the early days of the line, the loaded trains descended by gravity under control of a brakesman, horses hauling the trains of empties back to the summit. In 1865 the line was authorized to carry passengers, the trains then being hauled by small steam locomotives. Today, under preservation, with the use of the unique double-boiler locomotives, it is a major holiday attraction.

A station scene on the 15 inch narrow gauge railway at New Romney features locomotive no. 6 *Samson*, one of two locomotives of the Romney, Hythe and Dymchurch Railway built to the 4–8–2 wheel arrangement in 1921.

Clear road ahead as 4–8–2 no. 5 *Hercules* prepares to leave Hythe for New Romney in the 1950s. In 1928/9 the line was extended by 14 miles to Dungeness.

4–6–2 no. 3 *Southern Maid*, built in 1927, reposes outside the locomotive shed at New Romney.

A scene at Llanfair Caereinian in the early days of preservation features locomotive no. 1 on a typical goods train. Two locomotives named *The Earl* and *The Countess* worked the line in the heyday of the Welshpool and Llanfair Railway, both surviving to be preserved.

One of the original Tallylyn locomotives *Dolgoch* prepares to leave Towyn Wharf station on an idyllic afternoon in high summer.

A Fairlie Patent double bogie locomotive *Earl of Merioneth* built by the Ffestiniog Railway Co. at their Boston Lodge Works in 1979 pauses at Tan–Y–Bwlch on its journey from Porthmadog to Blaenau Ffestiniog.